Fastest Animals Of The World

Speedy Publishing LLC
40 E. Main St. #1156
Newark, DE 19711

www.speedypublishing.com

Copyright 2014
9781635012460
First Printed November 11, 2014

All Rights reserved. No part of this book may be reproduced or used in any way or form or by any means whether electronic or mechanical, this means that you cannot record or photocopy any material ideas or tips that are provided in this book.

speedypublishing

Speed Facts...

An adult bear can reach speeds of nearly 65 kilometres per hour. A grizzly has the speed to outrun a horse for a short distance.

Speed Facts...

The highest race speed recorded over two furlongs is 70.76 km/h (43.97 mph) and was achieved by Winning Brew trained by Francis Vitale (United States), at the Penn National Race Course, Grantville, Pennsylvania, United States, on 14 May 2008 according to the Guinness World Records.

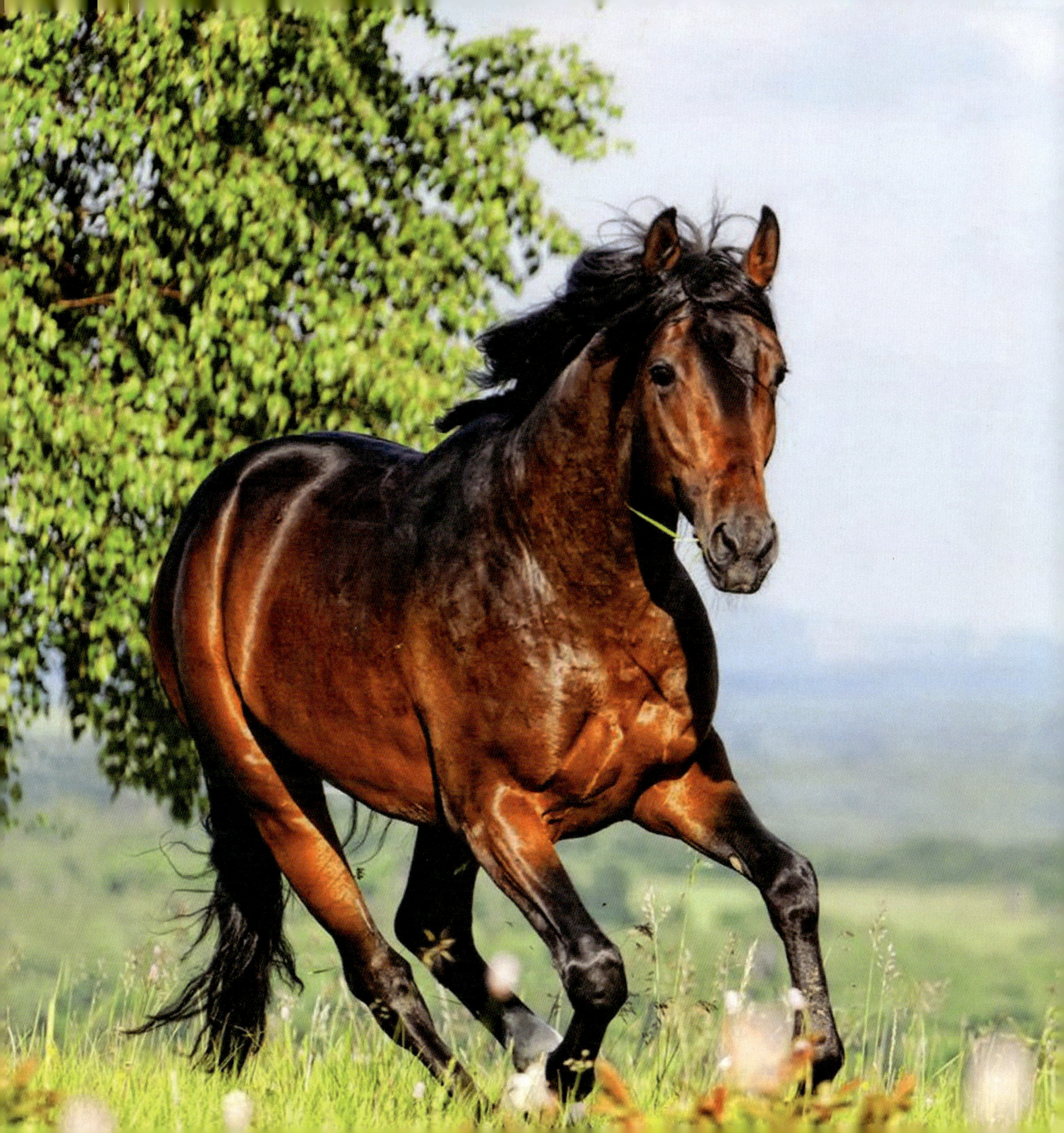

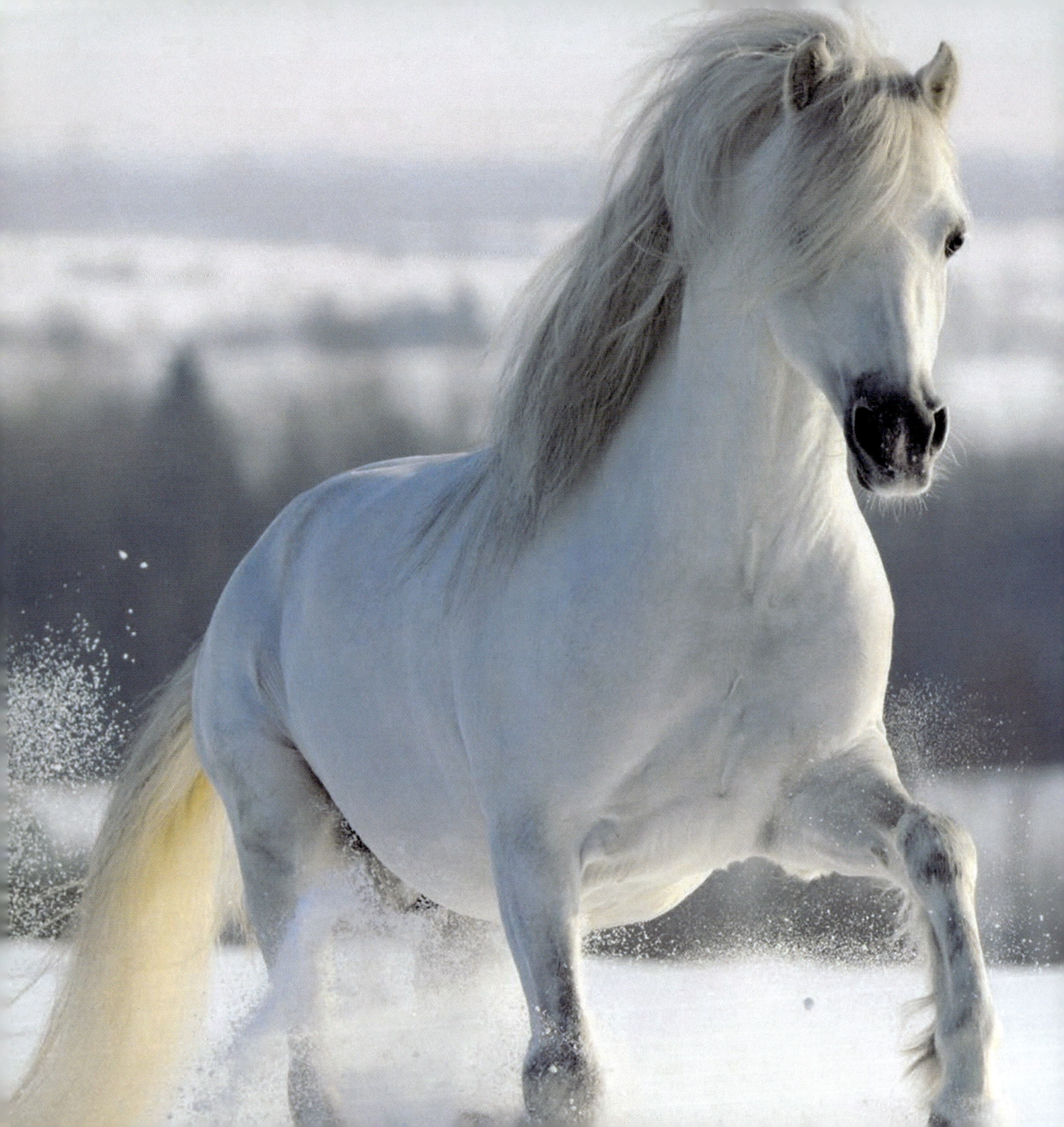

Speed Facts...

The so-called "natural" gaits, in increasing order of speed, are the walk, trot, canter, and gallop.

Speed Facts...

A spotted hyena can lope tirelessly for miles upon miles, can hit top speeds of 60kph, and can pursue prey for several kilometers at close to that top speed (50kph).

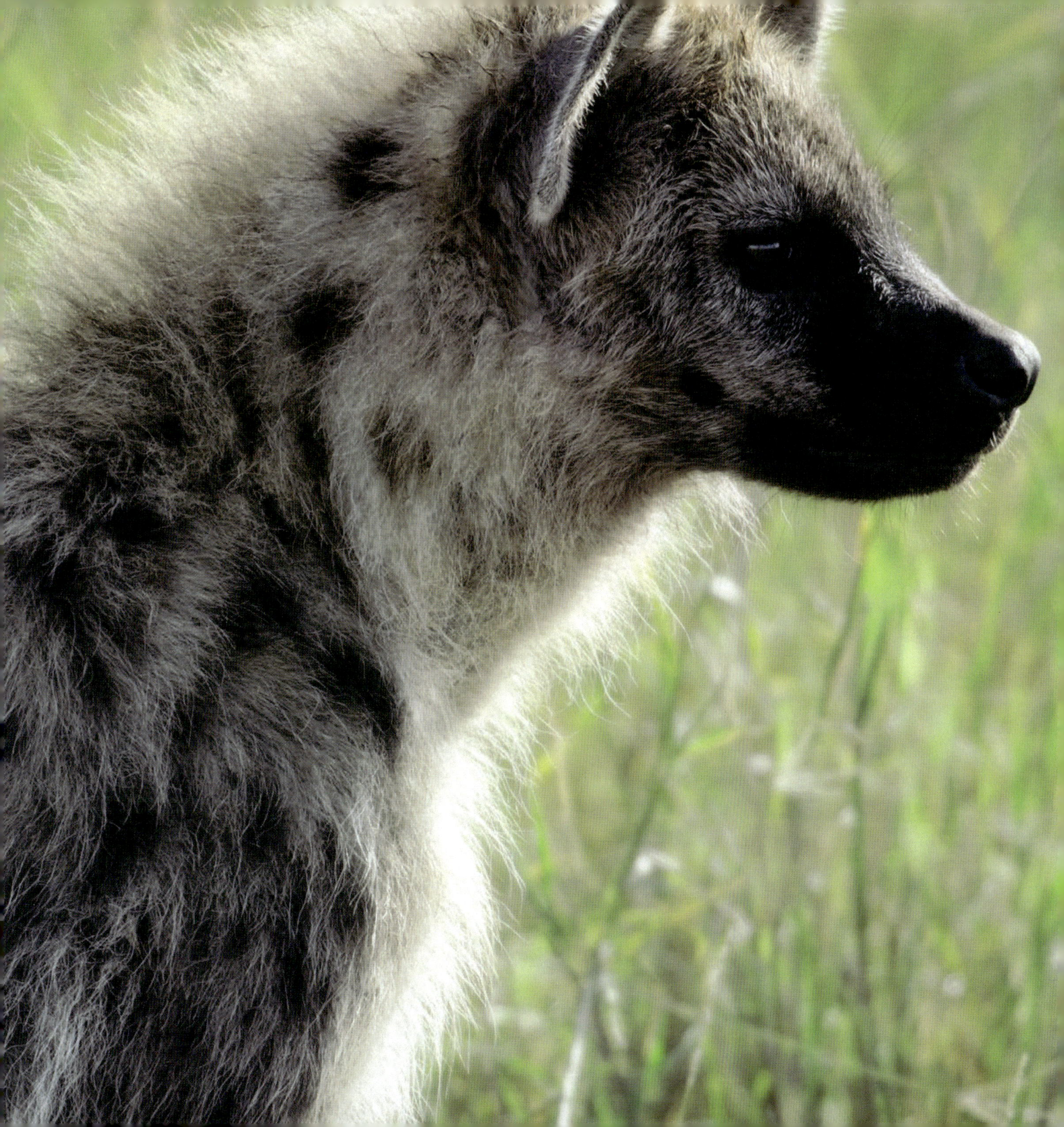

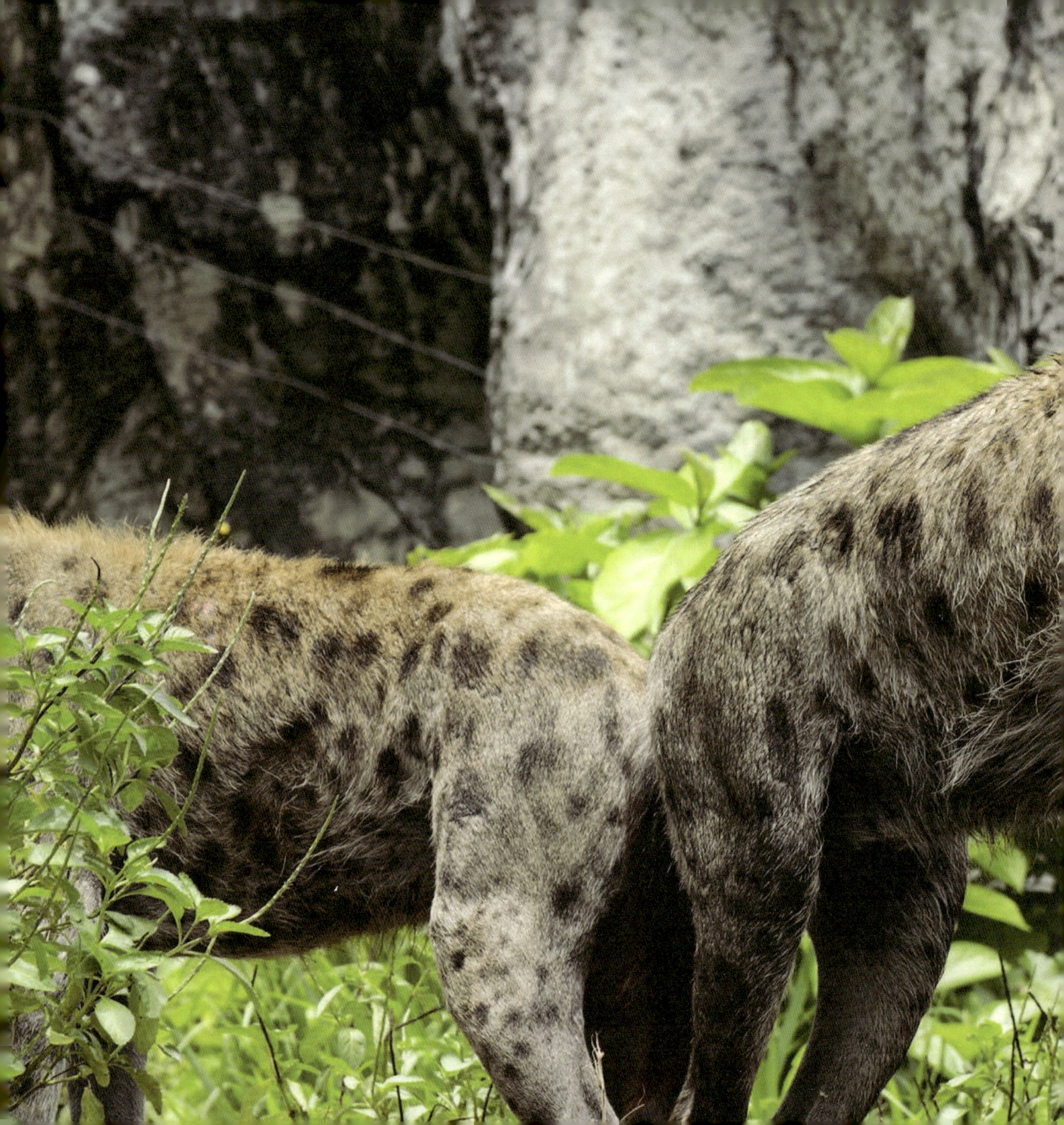

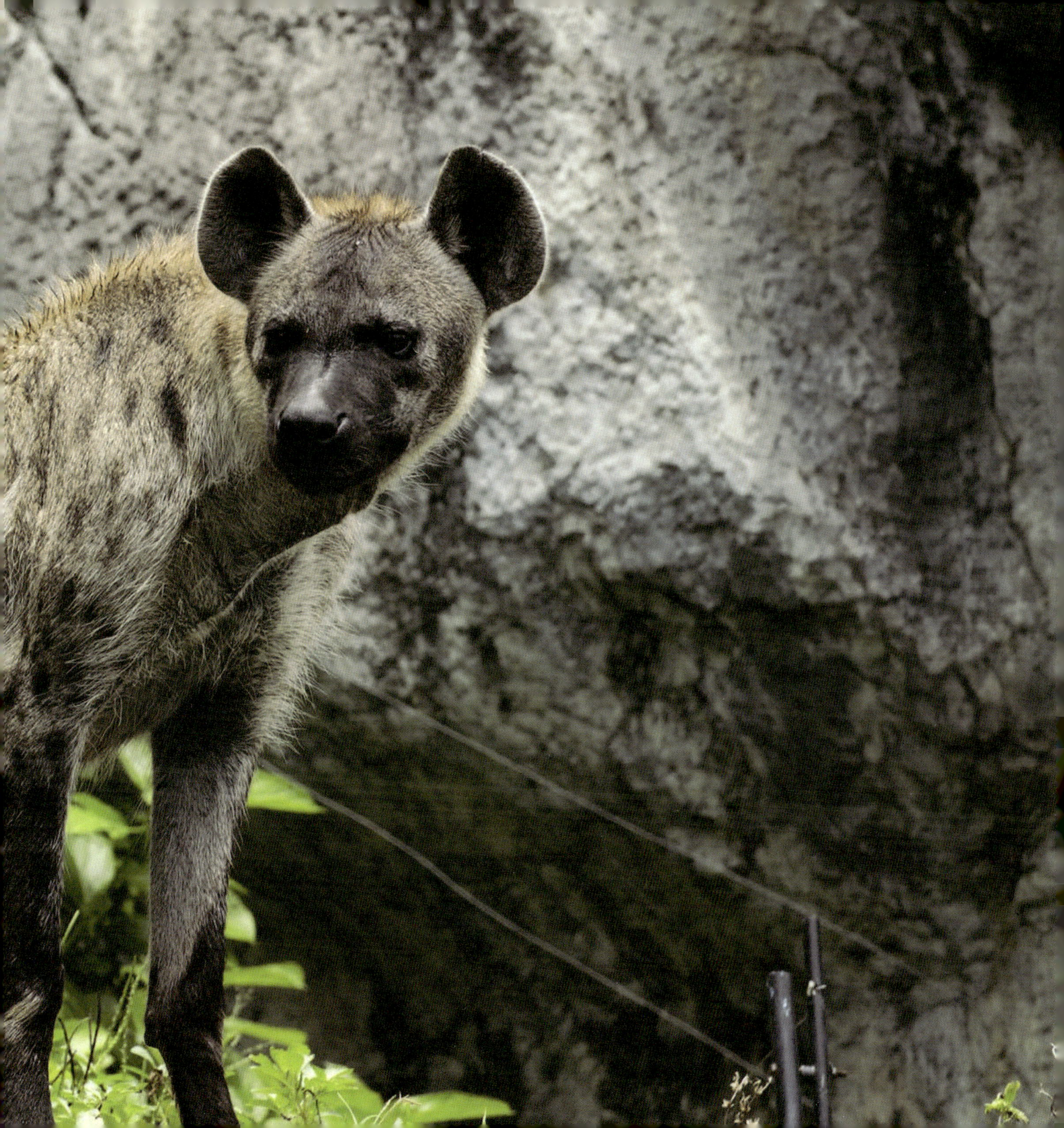

Speed Facts...

Despite their size tigers can reach speeds of 49 - 65 km/hr (35 - 40 mph) and they can leap 9 - 10 m (30 - 33 ft) in length and up to 5 m (16 ft) high.

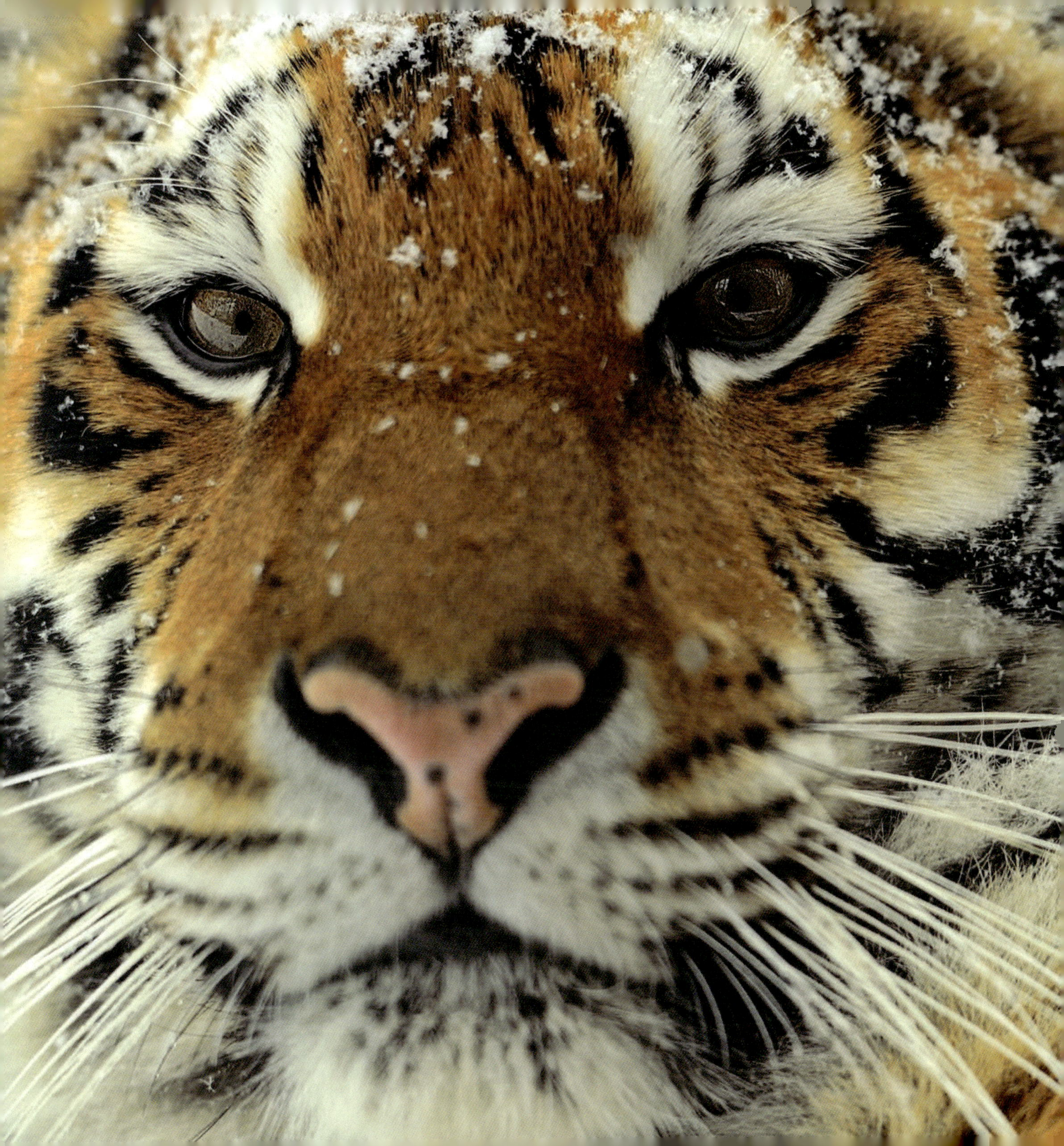

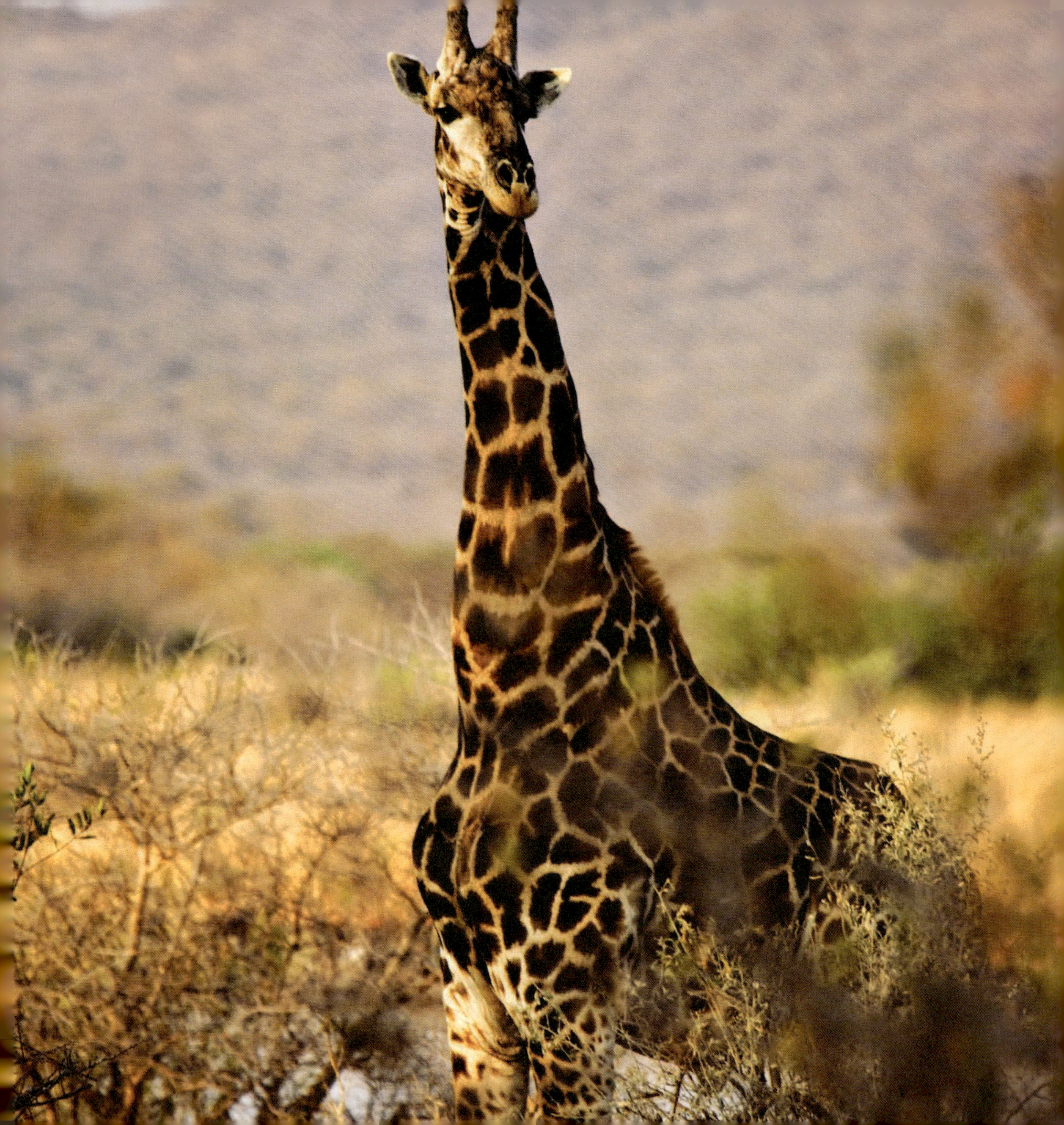

Speed Facts...

A giraffe, when running at full speed, can reach speeds of roughly 55 km/h. (About 34mph) Although, they will usually only run at this speed when being chased.

Speed Facts...

The Greyhound can reach a full speed of 70 kilometres per hour (43 mph) within 30 metres or six strides from the boxes, traveling at almost 20 metres per second for the first 250 metres of a race.

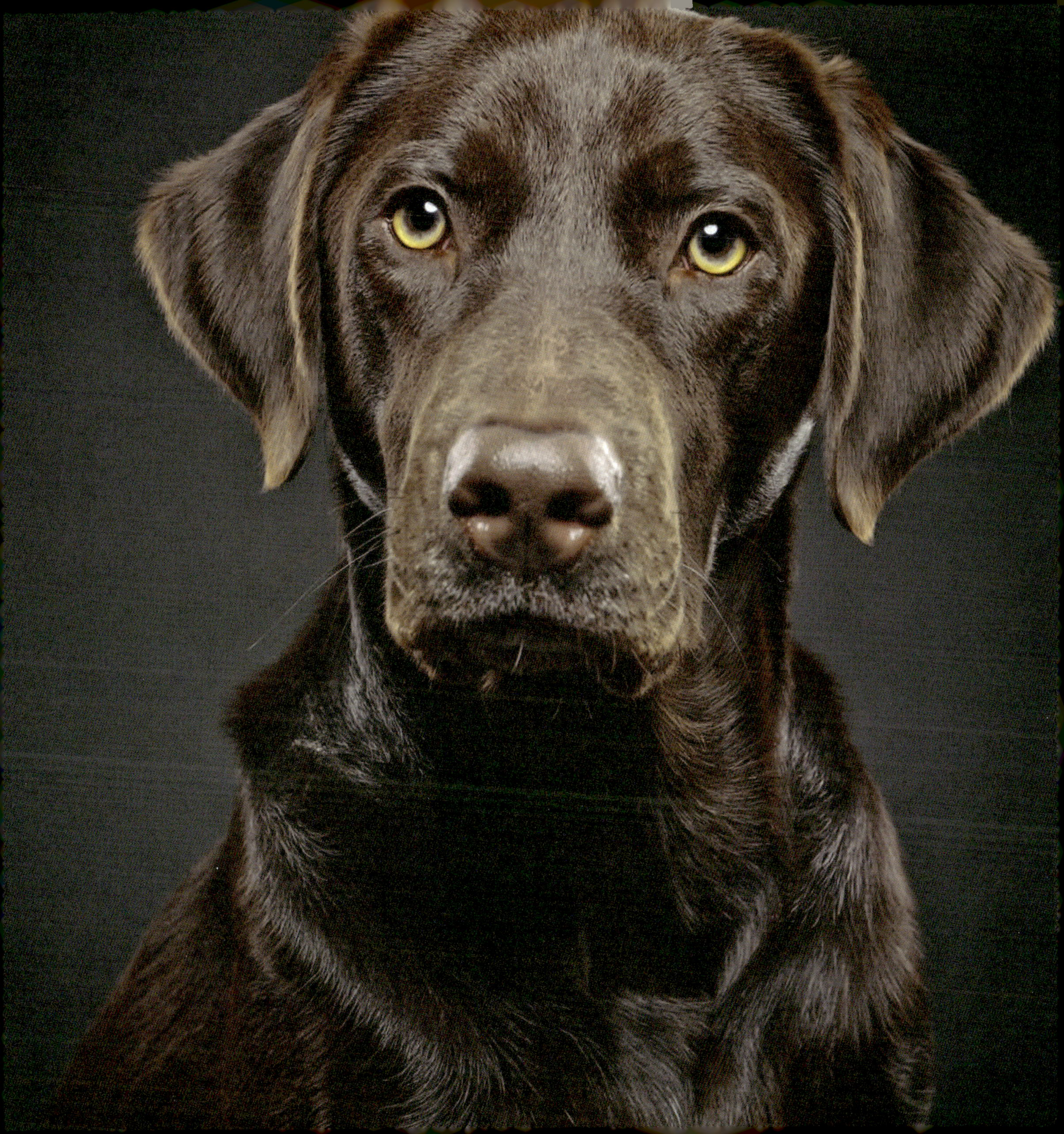

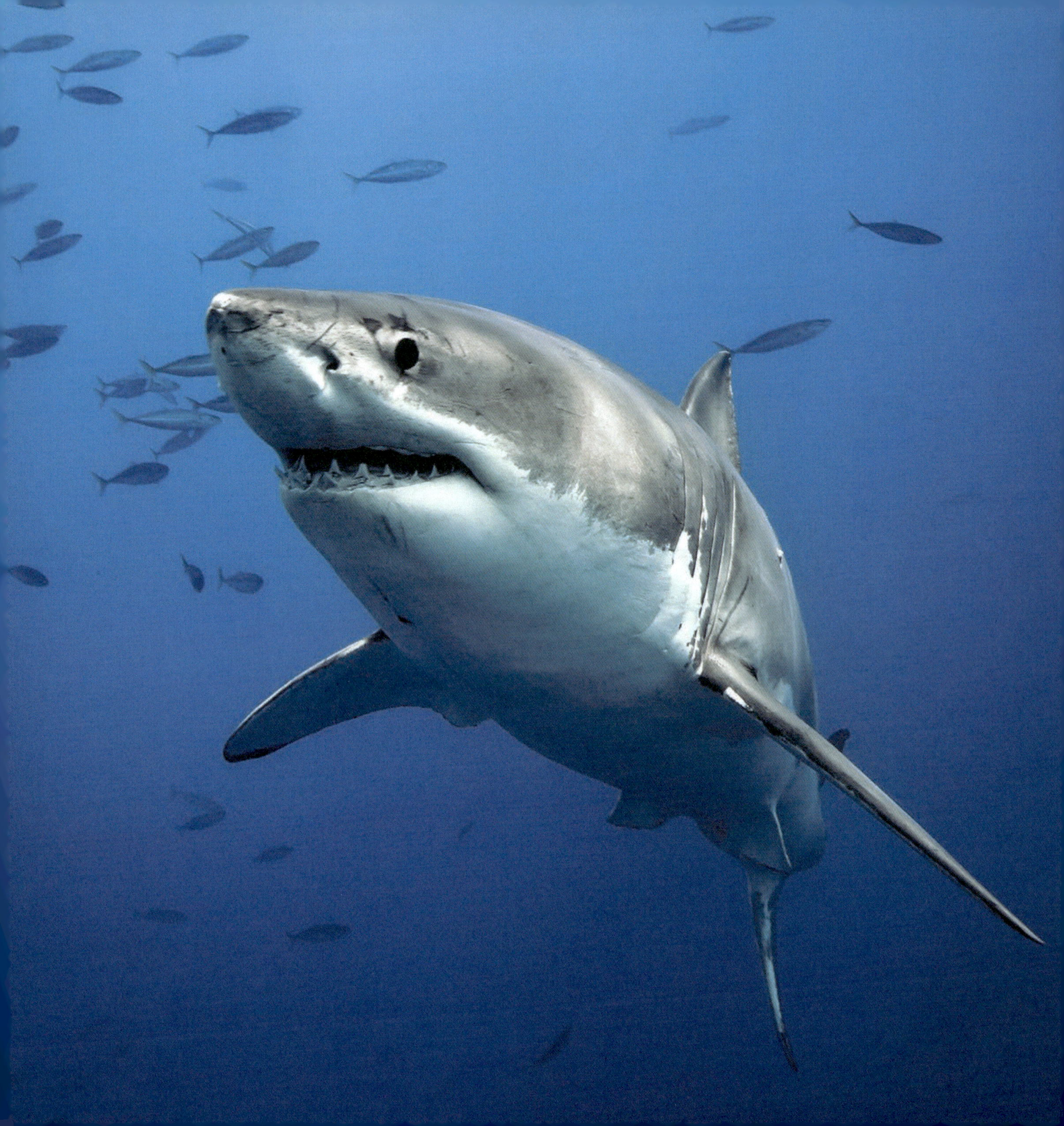

Speed Facts...

These sharks are very quick swimmers: They can swim at speeds of up to 15 mph (24 km/h), according to National Geographic.

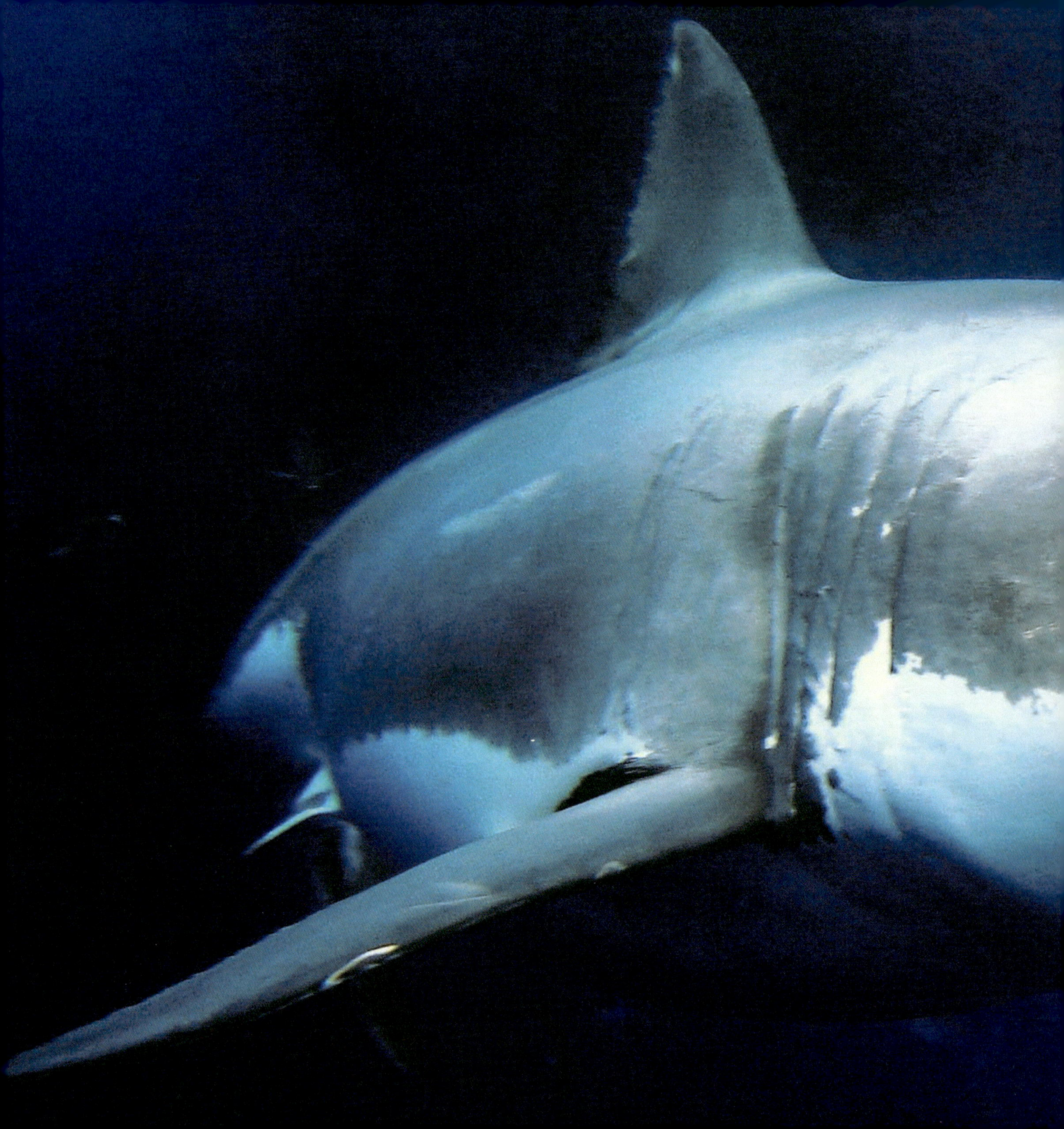

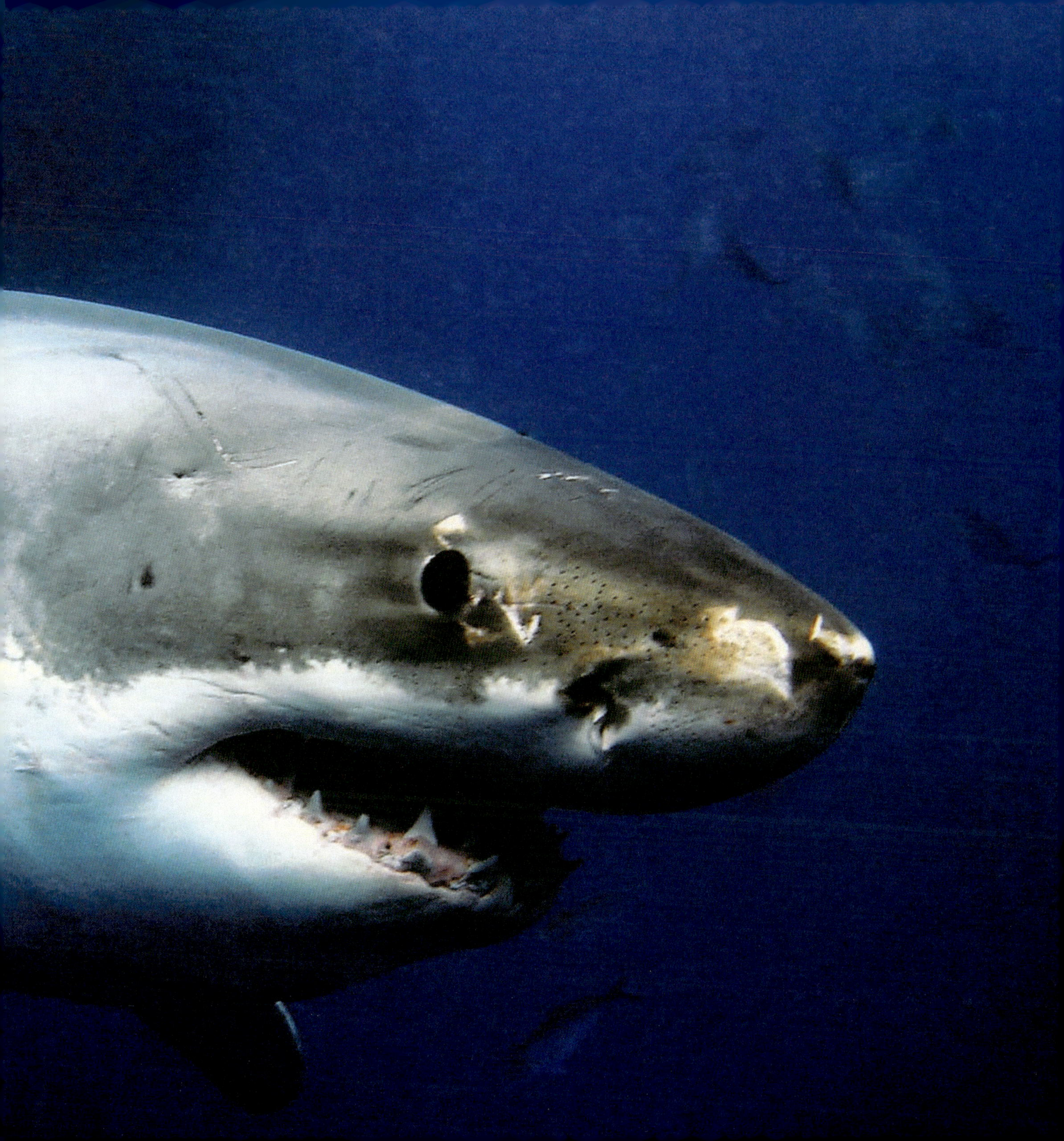

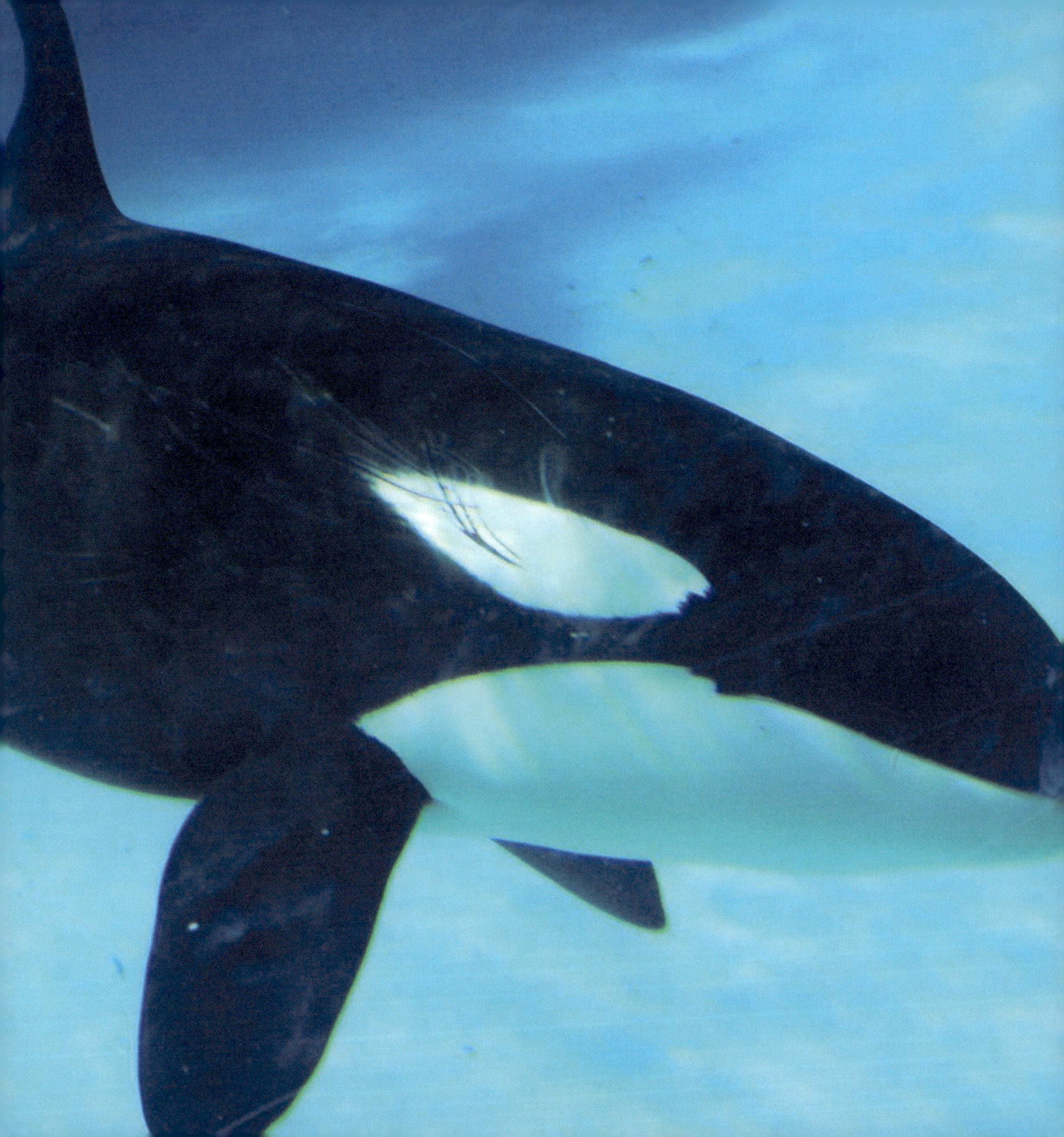

Speed Facts...

Orcas typically cruise around at about 3kn (6km/hr). If they have somewhere to go in a hurry they may travel at 6 or 7 kn (15km/hr). If need be, they can perform short, intense spurts of speeds up to 50km/hr.

Speed Facts...

Zebra can run up to 65km/h. They combine this fast running with excellent stamina and zig-zagging motions to try and evade predators that chase them.

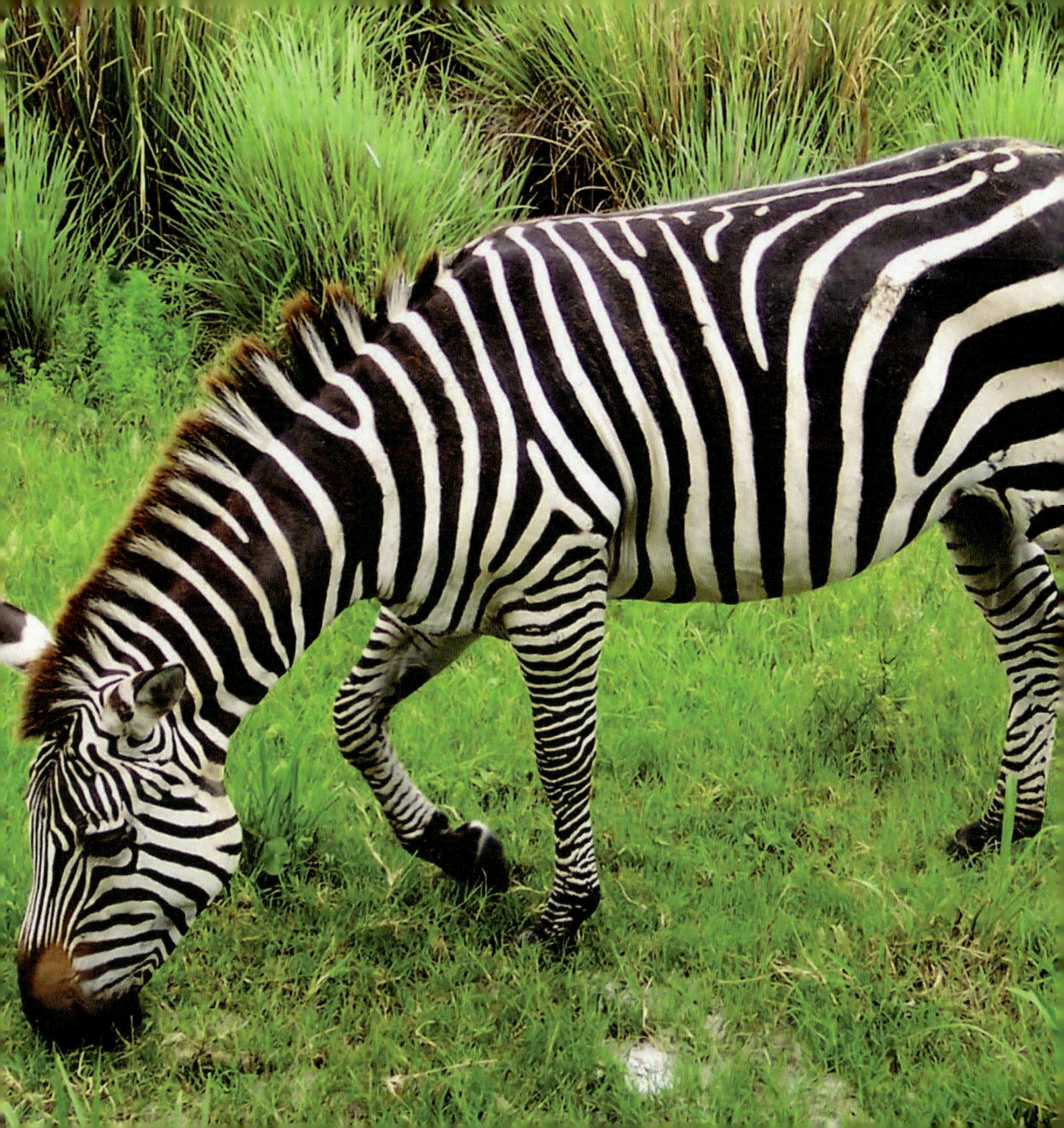

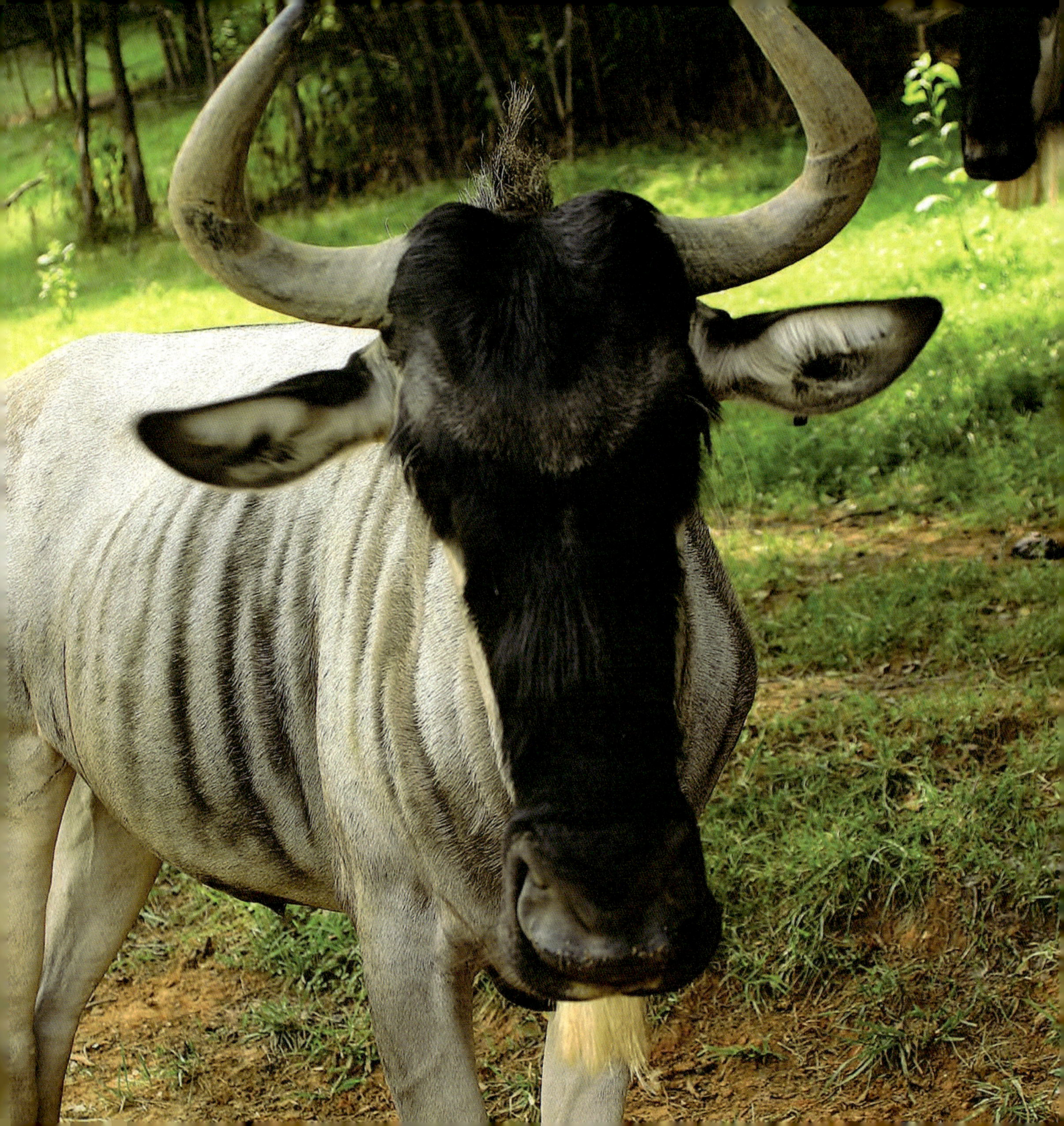

Speed Facts...

Wildebeest have a maximum running speed of around 80 km/h (50 mph). The primary defensive tactic is herding, where the young animals are protected by the older, larger ones, while the herd runs as a group.

Speed Facts...

Brown hares uses their powerful hind legs to escape predation by outrunning their enemies, and have been known to reach speeds of 72kph (45mph).

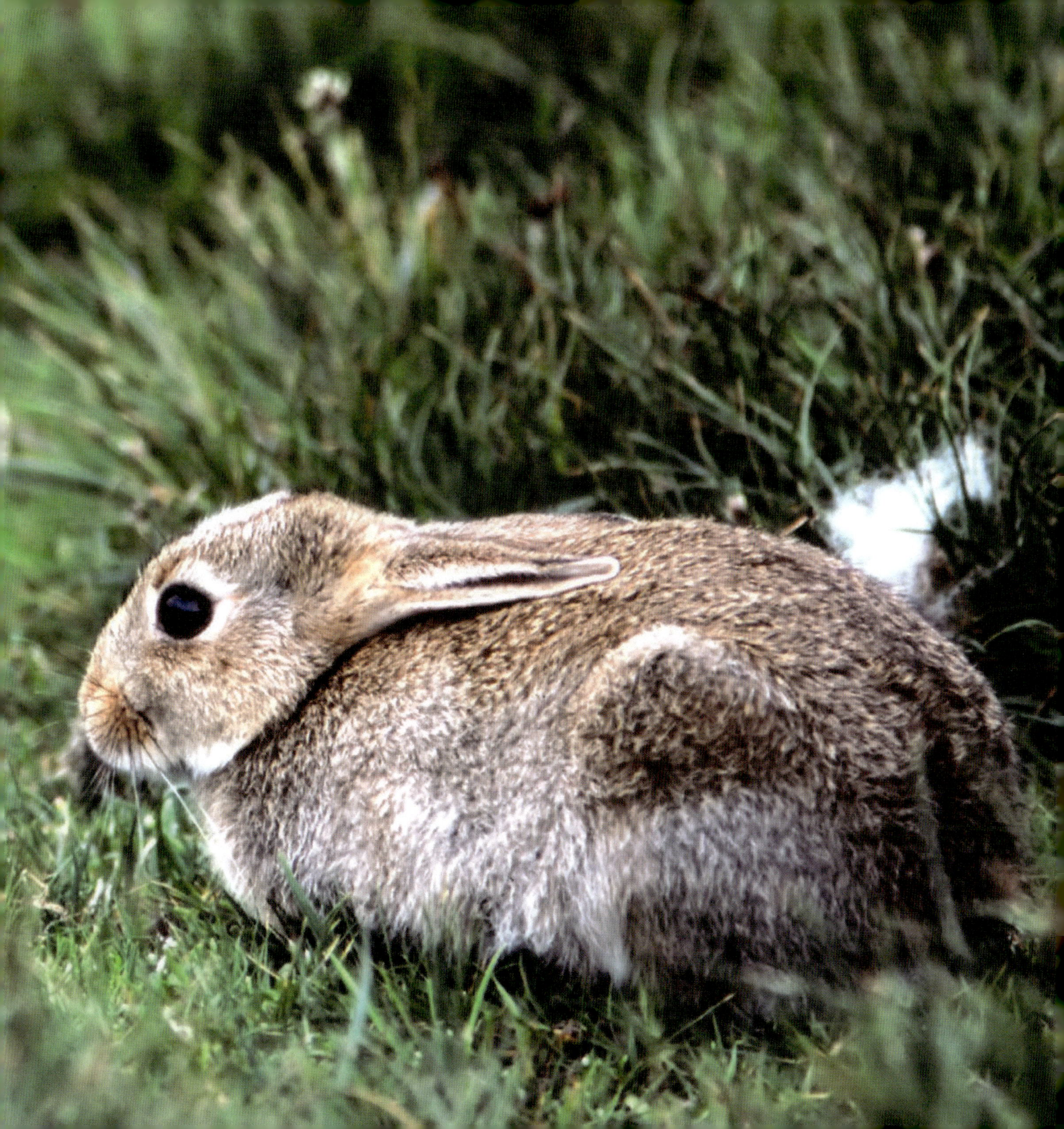

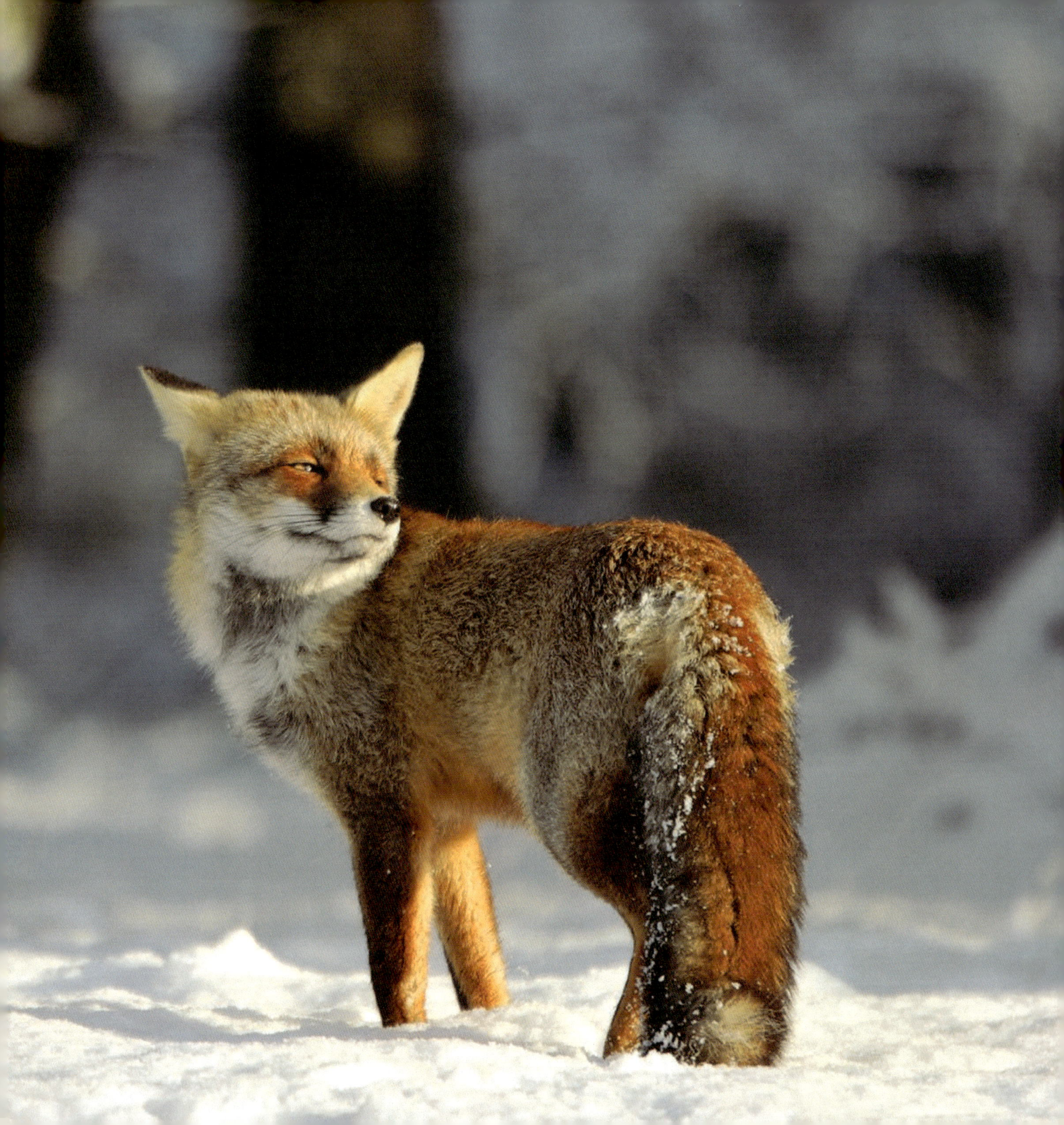

Speed Facts...

Red Foxes are very agile and they are able to run at speeds of up to 70 Km/h (45 mph).

Speed Facts...

Leopards are very agile and have been known to climb trees to store away captured prey. The highest speed that a leopard can reach is 60 kilometers or 37 miles per hour.

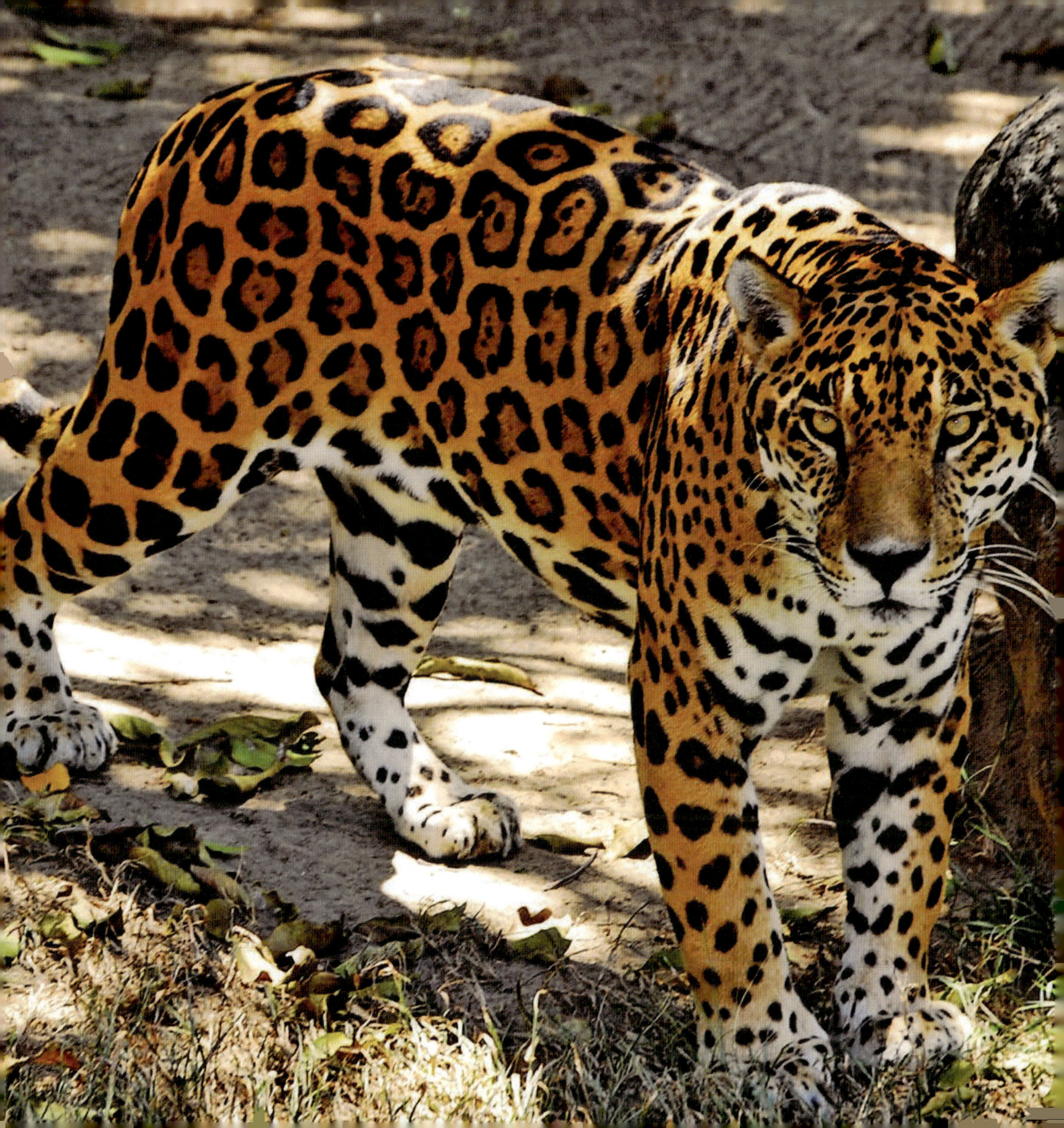

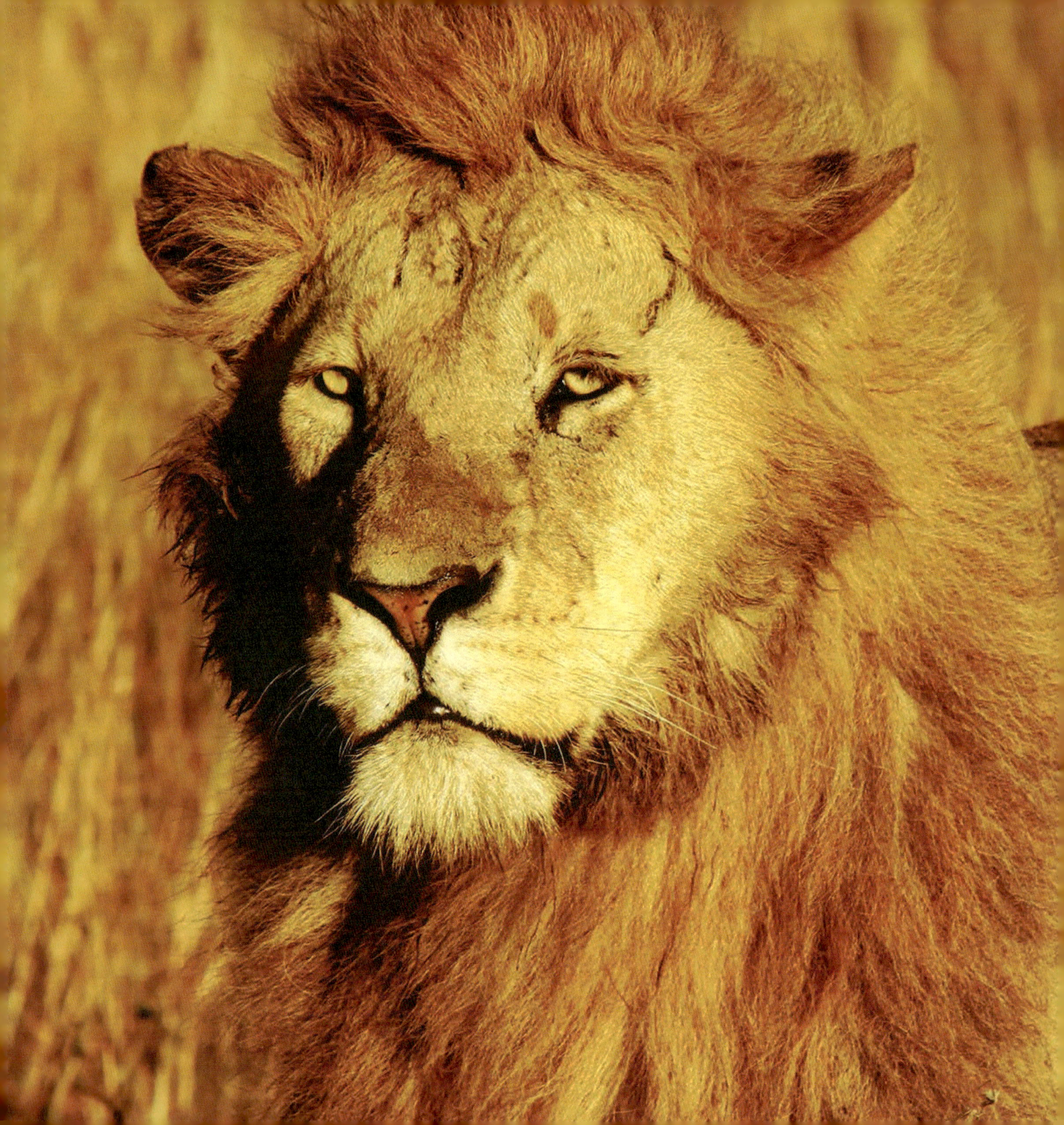

Speed Facts...

Lionesses can reach speeds of 81 km/h (50 mph), they only can do so for short bursts so they have to be close to their prey before starting the attack.

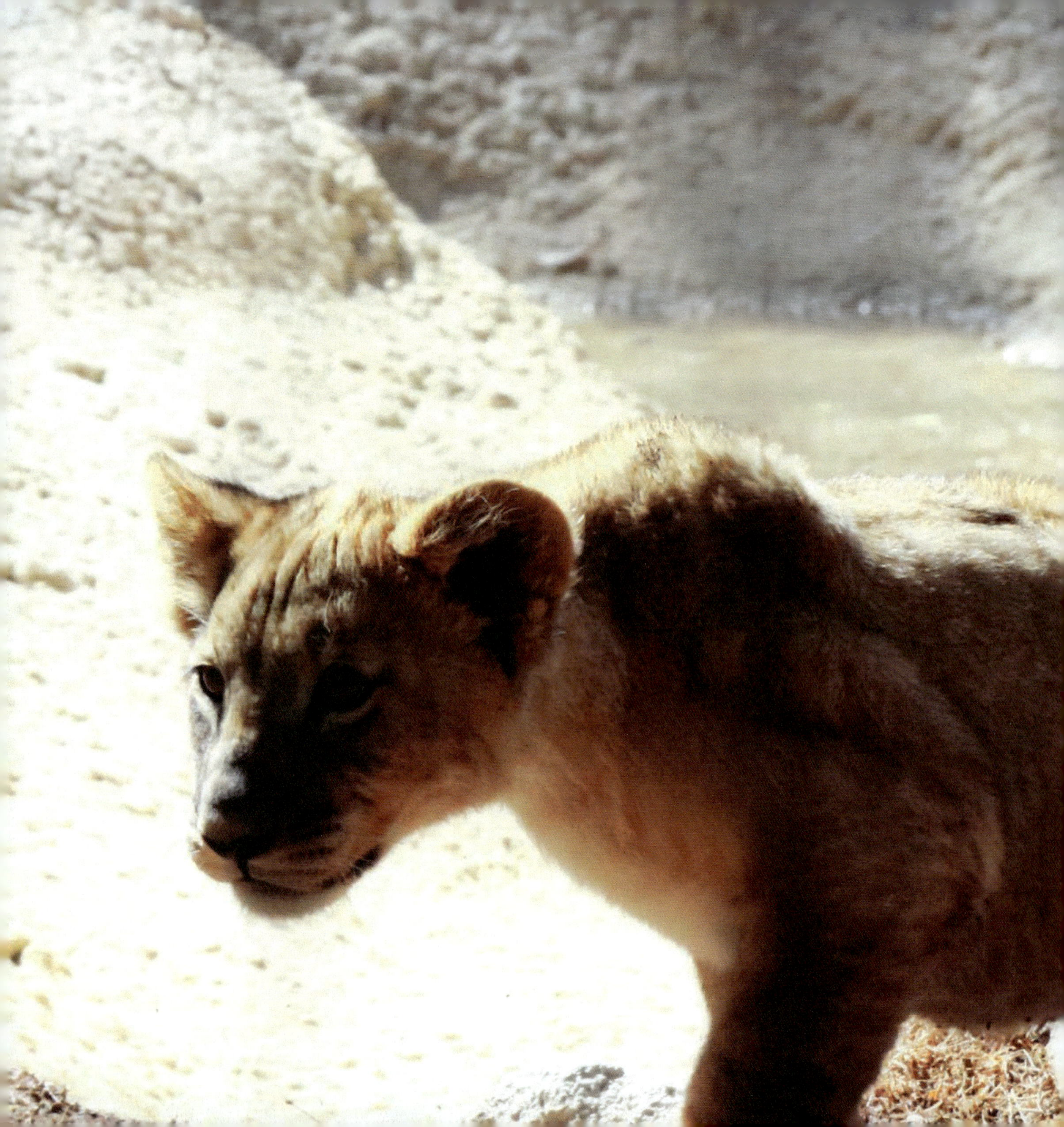

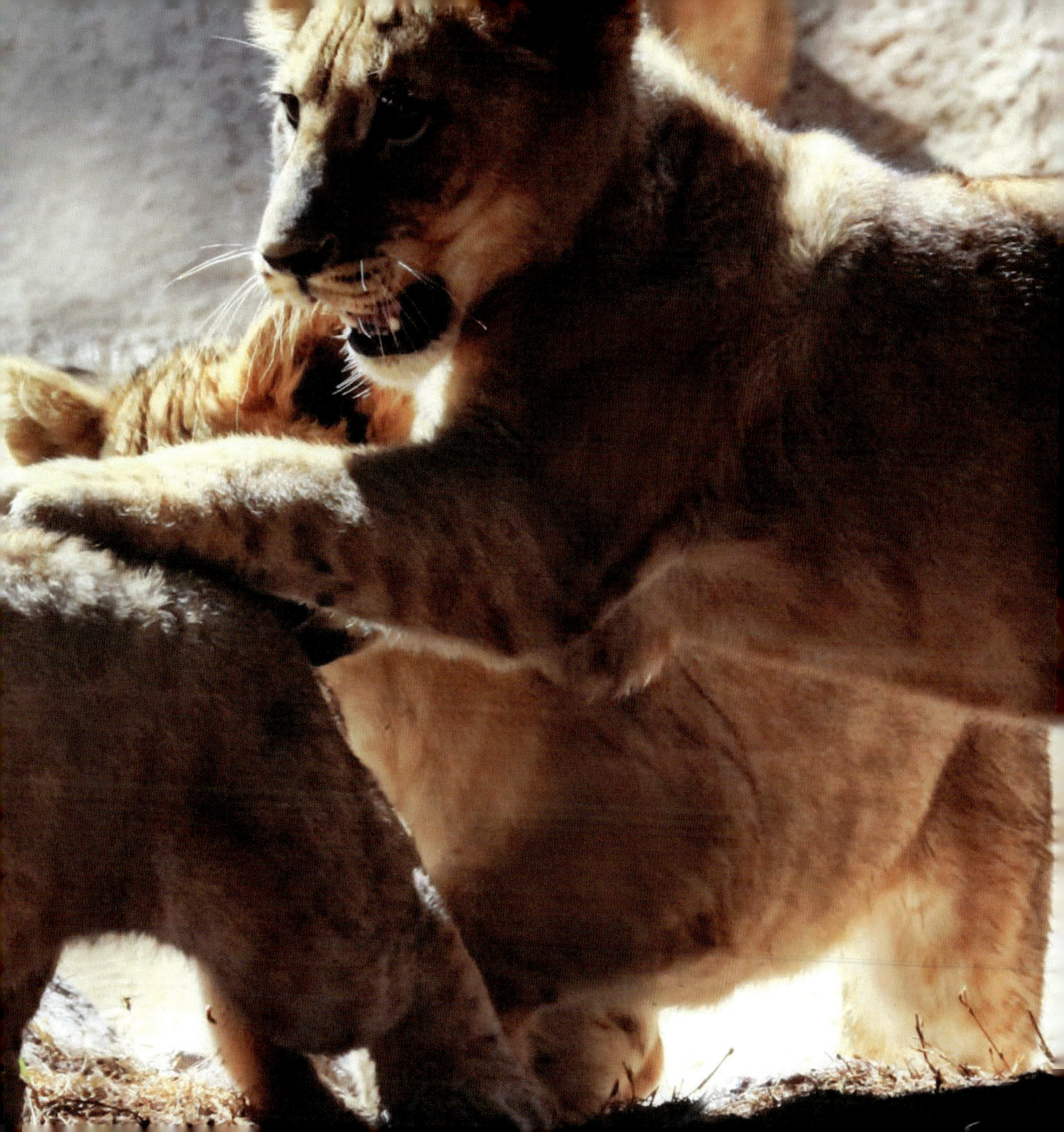

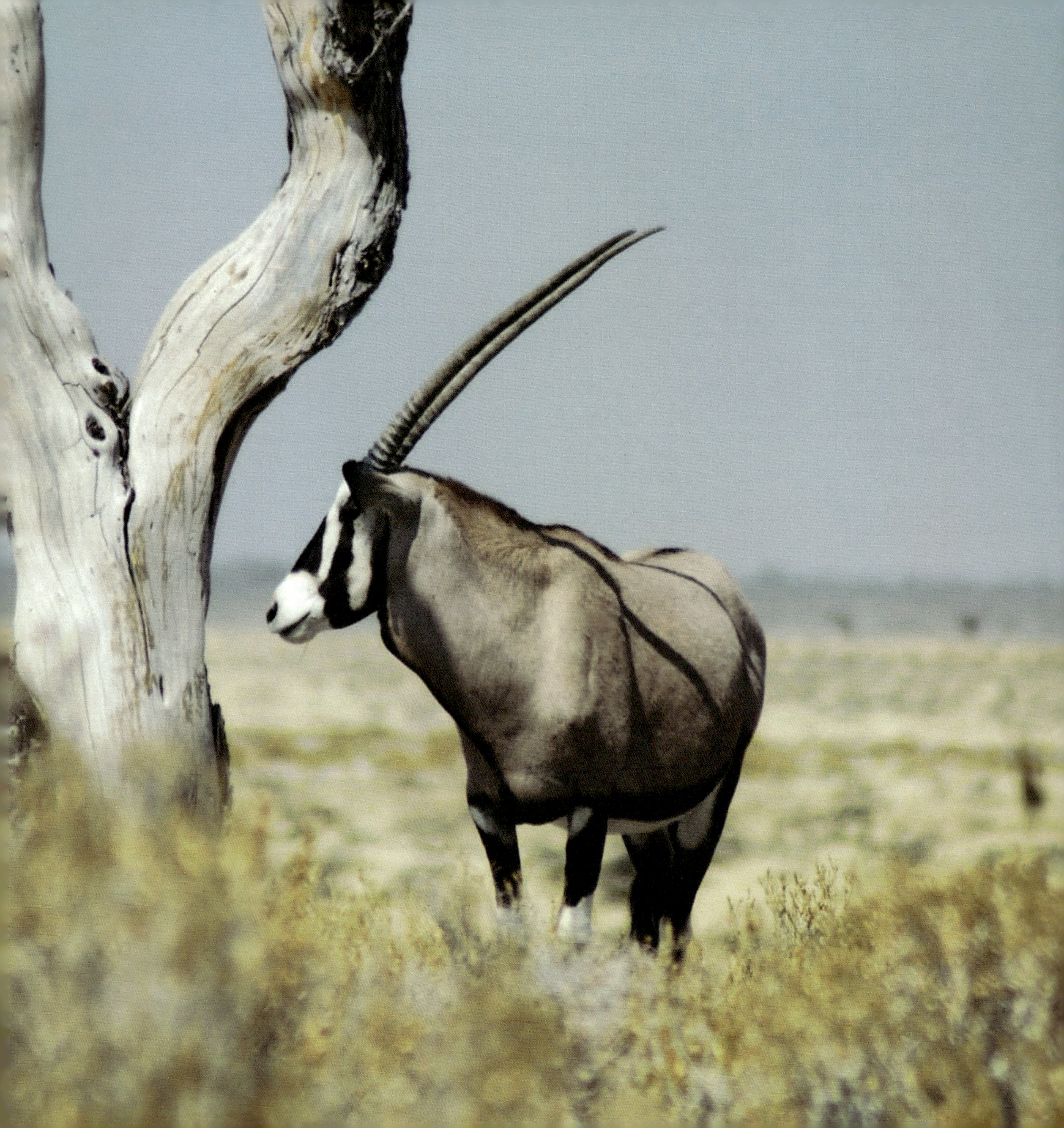

Speed Facts...

This small antelope-gazelle can run extremely fast, from 80 km/h (50 mph), to 96 km/h (60 mph) and zigzag, a peculiarity which often saves it from predators.

Speed Facts...

Elks can be quite large, but their size and build should not deceive you. The elk is capable of running at speeds as high as 45 miles per hour.

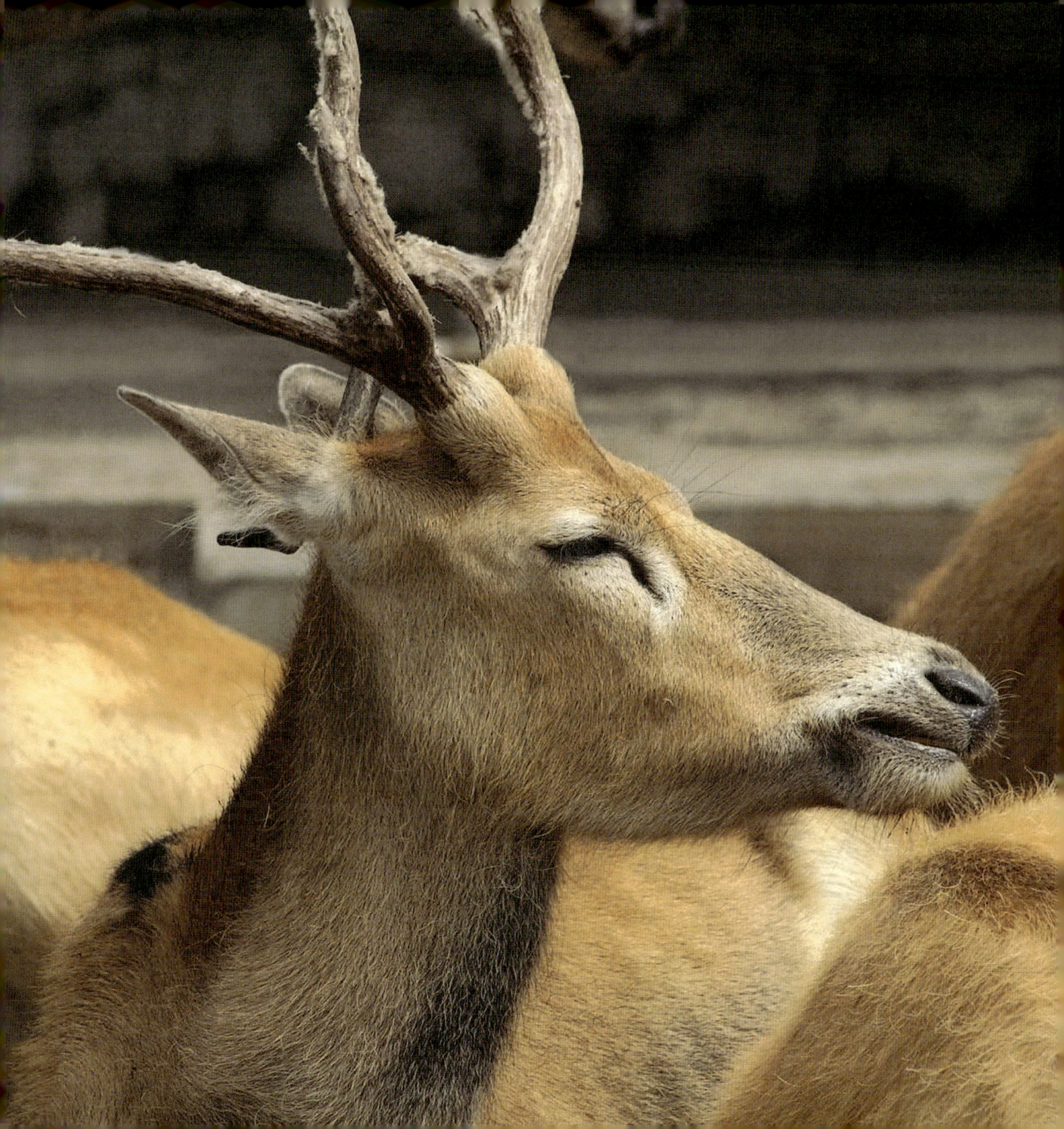

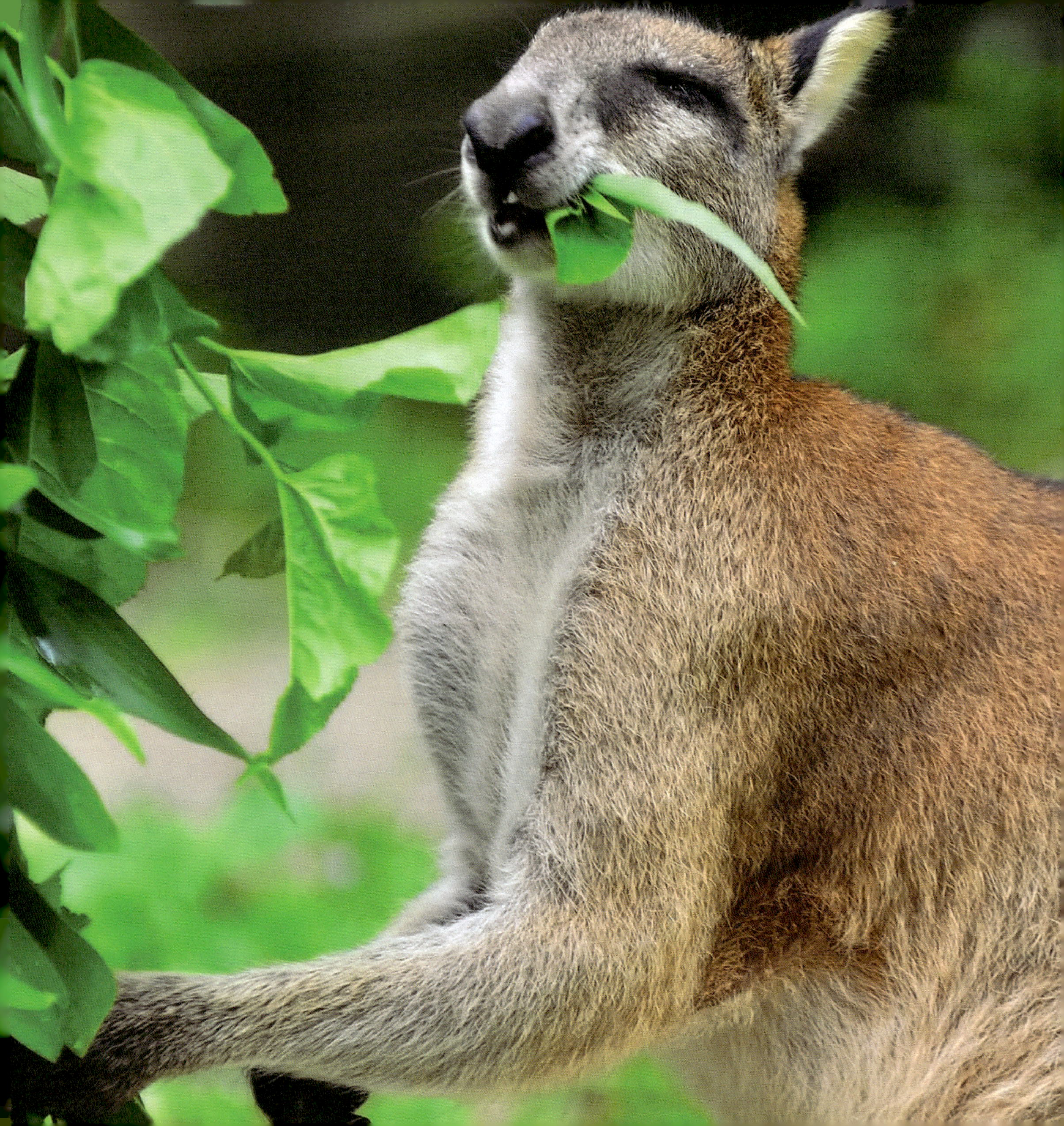

Speed Facts...

Kangaroos are the only large animals to use hopping as a means of locomotion. The comfortable hopping speed for Red Kangaroo is about 20–25 km/h (13–16 mph), but speeds of up to 70 km/h (44 mph) can be attained, over short distances, while it can sustain a speed of 40 km/h (25 mph) for nearly two kilometres.

Speed Facts...

The cheetah is the fastest land animal in the world. They can reach a top speed of around 113 km per hour. A cheetah can accelerate from 0 to 113 km in just a few seconds.

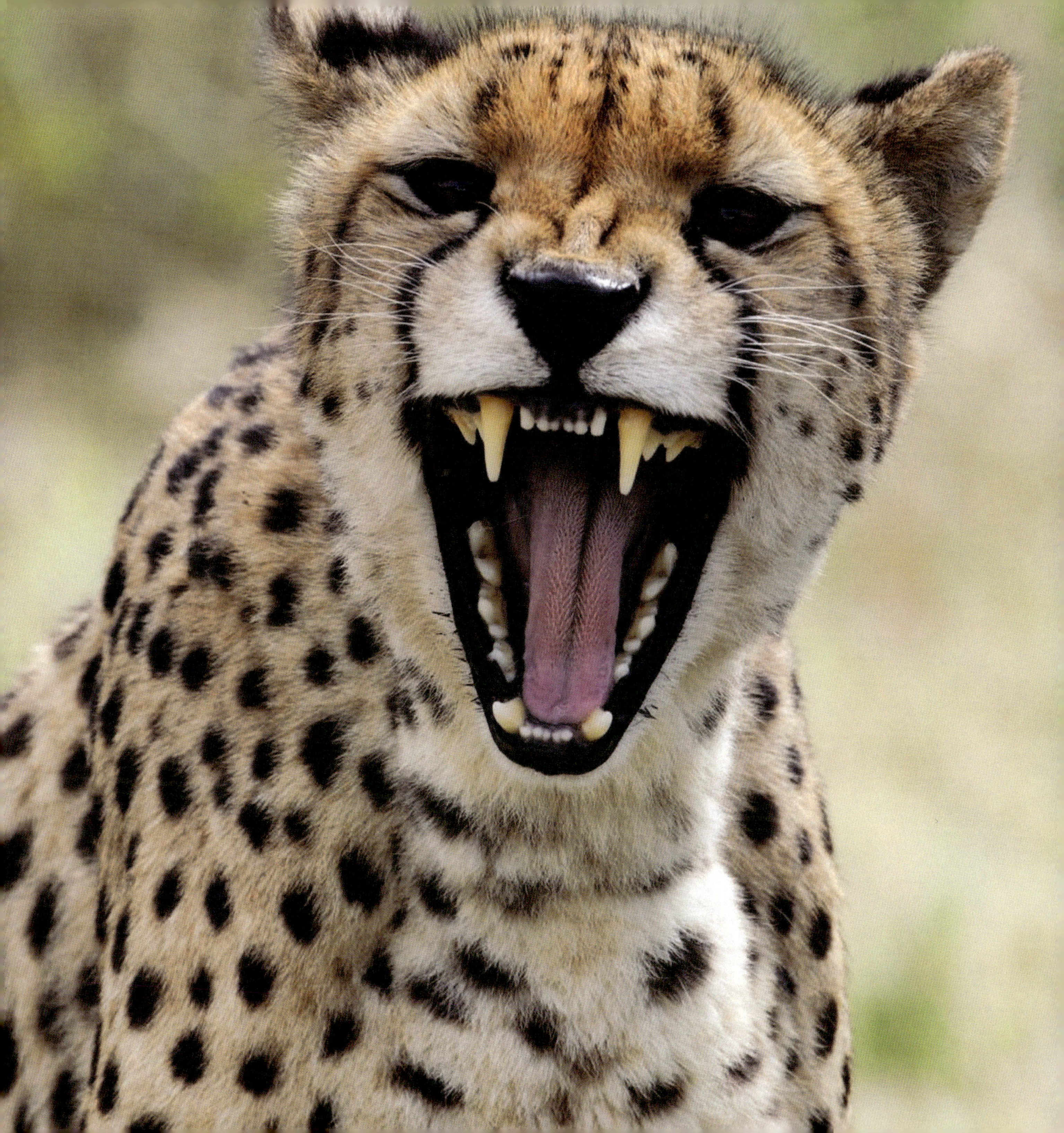

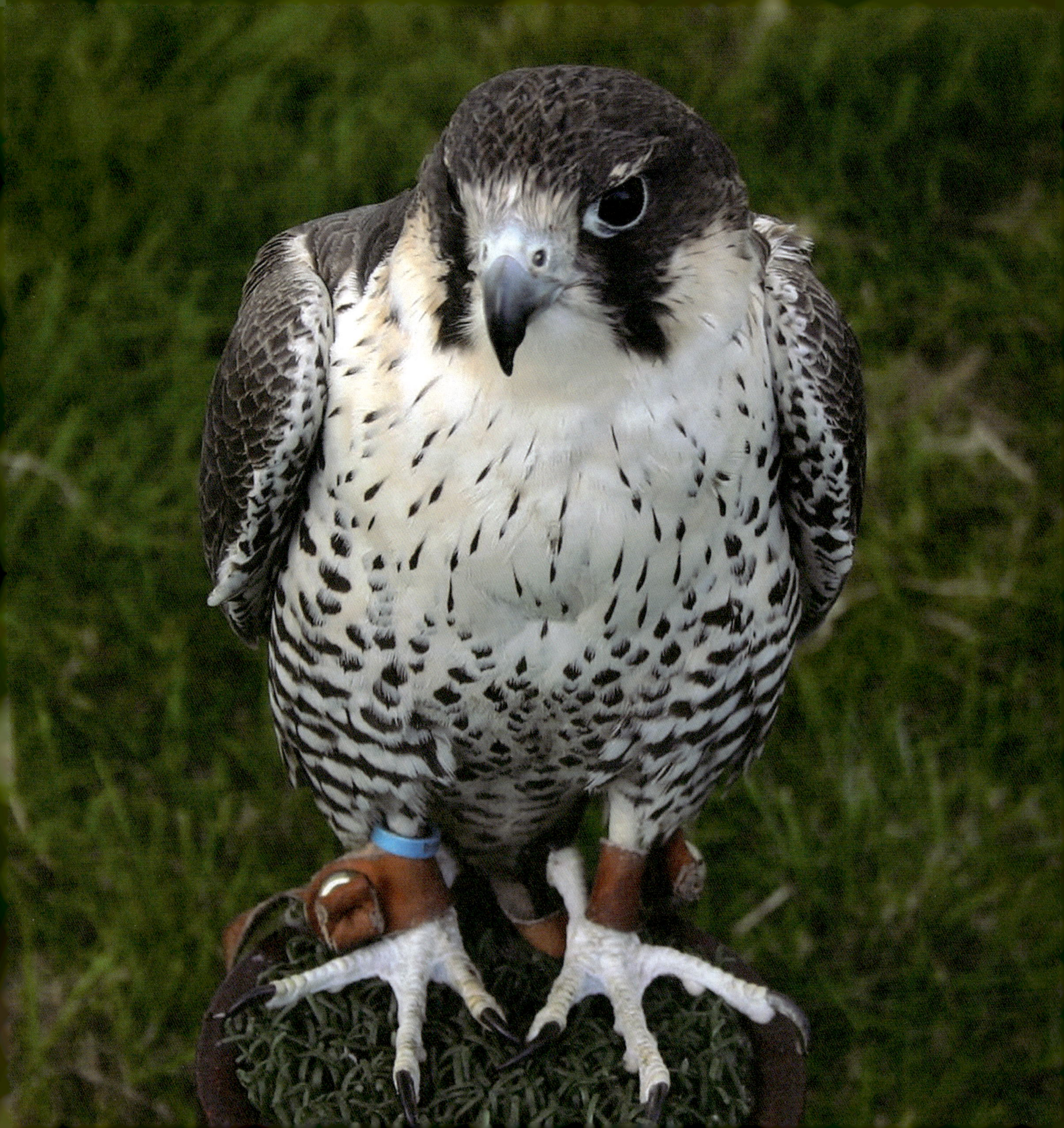

Speed Facts...

The peregrine falcon is renowned for its speed, reaching over 322 km/h (200 mph) during its characteristic hunting stoop (high speed dive), making it the fastest member of the animal kingdom.

Printed in Great Britain
by Amazon